Dogs of the World

DOT-TO-DOT

Connect the Dots & Color

Marty Crisp

Illustrated by Nancy Harrison

Sterling Publishing Co., Inc.
New York

To my Dad, Charles Morris Tibbels, who taught me how to connect life's dots. As a father and a man, he is a breed apart.

I used dozens of reference books and other sources to come up with amazing facts and basic data on the 38 breeds in this book, but I'd especially like to acknowledge Desmond Morris, former curator of mammals at the London Zoo and the foremost authority on dogs today.

10   9   8   7   6   5   4   3   2   1

Published by Sterling Publishing Co., Inc.
387 Park Avenue South, New York, NY 10016
© 2005 by Marty Crisp
Distributed in Canada by Sterling Publishing
$^c/o$ Canadian Manda Group, 165 Dufferin Street
Toronto, Ontario, Canada M6K 3H6
Distributed in Great Britain and Europe by Chris Lloyd at Orca Book
Services, Stanley House, Fleets Lane, Poole BH15 3AJ, England
Distributed in Australia by Capricorn Link (Australia) Pty. Ltd.
P.O. Box 704, Windsor, NSW 2756, Australia

Illustrated by Nancy Harrison

Printed in China

Sterling ISBN 1-4027-1048-8

CONTENTS

AIREDALE

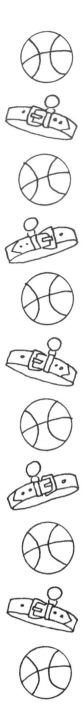

ORIGIN:	Great Britain, 1800s
SIZE:	22–24 inches (56–61cm) tall; weighing 44–50 pounds (20–23kg)
APPEARANCE:	Small, dark eyes; long, square face; drop ears; long tail, carried high; alert and fearless

Developed to hunt badgers and otters, Airedales are the largest of all terriers. They're named for a district in Yorkshire, England (where the smallest of all terriers, the Yorkie, was also first bred), and come from the mixing of now extinct Black-and-Tan Terriers with Otter Hounds to create a terrier with size and strength.

Although bred for otter hunting, Airedales are versatile dogs also used for duck hunting, ratting, deer tracking, and guard dog duties. Plucky and tireless, the Airedale won't start a fight, but once involved in one, it will fight to the death to protect its home and family.

DID YOU KNOW? During World War I, a British army dog named Airedale Jack saved his whole battalion by delivering a note pleading for reinforcements through a storm of enemy fire. Jack died soon after he completed his 4-mile (6km) journey.

AMERICAN FOXHOUND

ORIGIN: The U.S. South, 1700s.

SIZE: 21–25 inches (53–64cm); weighing 65–75 pounds (29–34kg)

APPEARANCE: Short coat, drop ears

Active and friendly, American Foxhounds have a songlike voice that has been incorporated into recorded music. The dogs were created almost entirely by the first president of the United States, George Washington. A keen hunter, Washington crossed English Foxhounds, imported to the United States back in the 1650s, with French Foxhounds, given to him by General Lafayette after the Revolutionary War. That makes Washington both the father of his country and the father of the American Foxhound!

DID YOU KNOW? The largest fully surviving litter of puppies ever born, according to the Guinness Book of World Records, was a litter of 23 pups born to an American Foxhound in Ambler, Pennsylvania, in 1944.

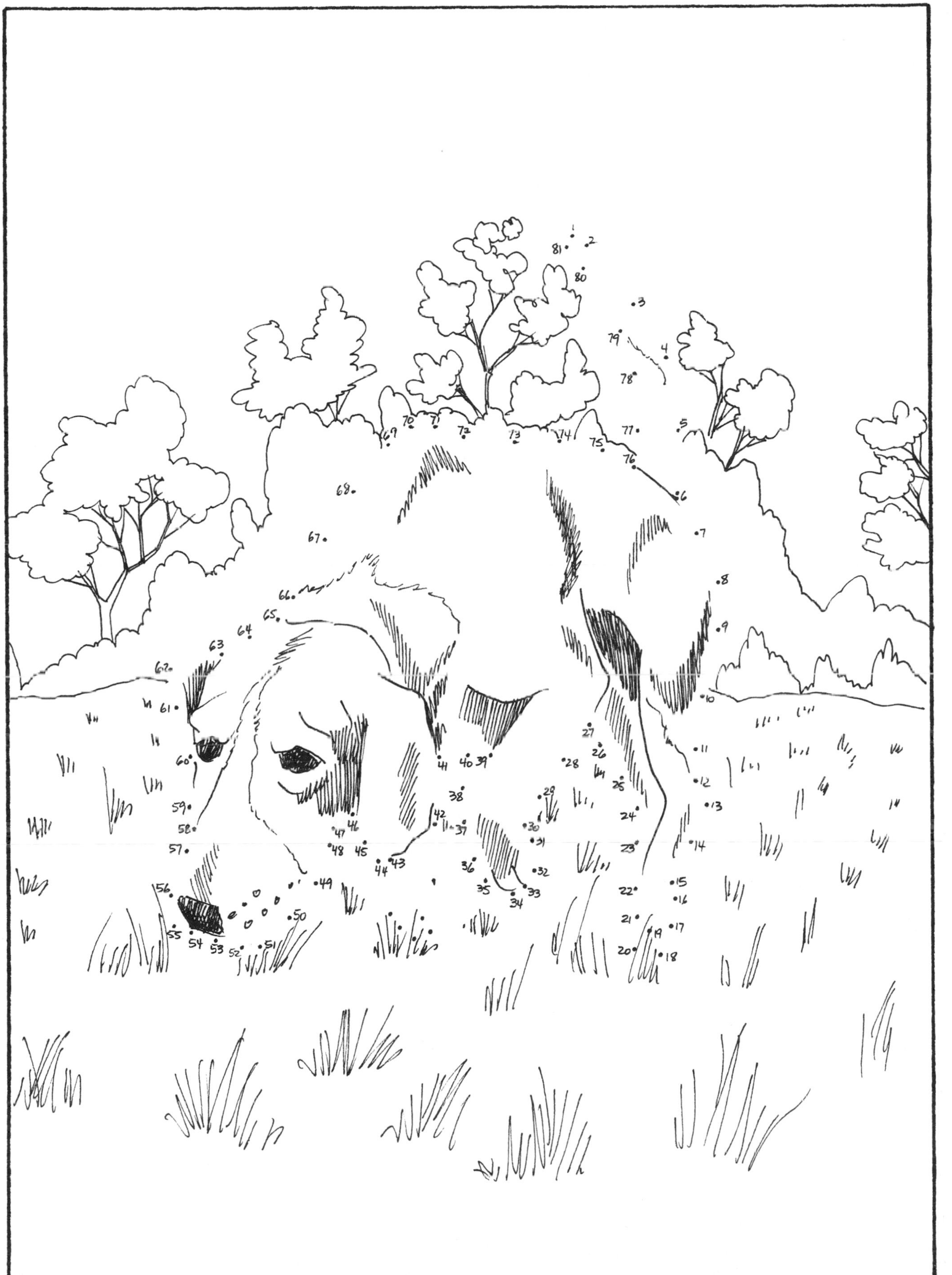

AUSTRALIAN KELPIE

ORIGIN:	Australia, 1870
SIZE:	17–20 inches (43–51cm) tall; weighing 25–45 pounds (11–20kg)
APPEARANCE:	Pricked ears; small feet; foxlike face; short, dense undercoat with glossy, weather-resistant outer coat.

The owner of a New South Wales cattle station imported a pair of English Collies in 1870, to help control his widely scattered cattle. The Collies mated aboard ship during the long ocean voyage from England, and their offspring was bred to a local black-and-tan, part-Dingo dog named Kelpie.

Extremely smart and responsive, Kelpies now herd both cattle and sheep; a well-trained Kelpie can do the herding work of six men, and travel 40 miles (64km) a day. When herding sheep, they often walk across the backs of their charges to get where they're going. Some people say Kelpies mesmerize or hypnotize sheep simply by staring at them.

DID YOU KNOW? An Australian Kelpie named Bluey herded cattle for an amazing 20 years after his birth in 1910. Bluey finally retired, but lived on, dying in 1939 at the age of 29½, the oldest dog in recorded history.

BASENJI

ORIGIN:	The Congo (now Zaire), 1500s or earlier
SIZE:	16–17 inches (41–43cm) tall; weighing 21–24 pounds (10–11kg).
APPEARANCE:	Distinctive tail curling over the rump; wrinkled foreheads (which create a perpetually worried look).

These terrierlike dogs are depicted on the tombs of Egyptian pharaohs, but were fully developed in Zaire dating back to at least the 1500s. Basenji is an African word meaning "bush thing."

Trained as bush hunters by pygmy tribes, these "barkless" dogs make a sound often described as a yodel—a sort of chortling call that reminds some people of a deep laugh. They're curious, playful, and gentle. Basenjis are also the only canines that groom their short coats with their tongues, like cats.

DID YOU KNOW? Basenjis don't walk the way most dogs do. Their gait resembles the trot of a thoroughbred horse, a two-beat gait in which the right front and left rear legs move in synchrony. Most dogs move the front and hind legs on the same side in unison.

BASSET HOUND

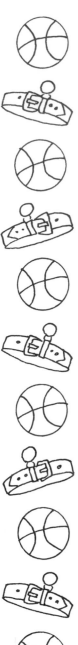

ORIGIN:	France, 1600s
SIZE:	13–15 inches (33–34cm) tall; weighing 40–60 pounds (18–27kg)
APPEARANCE:	Short legs; long body, ears, and tail; big head

Relative to size, the Basset is the heaviest-boned dog in the canine world. With their short legs and long bodies, some people say bassets look almost like big dogs that have been chopped off at the knees.

The name Basset comes from the French word *bas*, meaning "low." Independent and active, even though they look a bit slow and ponderous, Bassets were once used for rabbit hunting, but are now mainly companion dogs. Their short legs usually have a wrinkled appearance.

DID YOU KNOW? A Basset Hound is the trademarked logo for a popular brand of American suede shoes called Hush Puppies.

BEAGLE

ORIGIN: Great Britain, 1300s

SIZE: 13–16 inches (33–41cm) tall; weighing 18–30 pounds (8–14kg)

APPEARANCE: Long floppy ears; upright tail

First bred for hunting rabbits, these small hound dogs have both Foxhound and terrier genes in their ancestry. More than most dogs, Beagles work in packs, pursuing their quarry by scent with remarkable stamina and tenacity. Although it no longer exists, a miniature Beagle, called a Pocket Beagle was popular in the first half of the 20th century. It grew to be no more than 9 inches (23cm) tall.

DID YOU KNOW? The Beagle Brigade sniffs out contraband fruit and plants illegally brought into the United States at international airports. Chosen by the U.S. government for their excellent noses and gentle natures, Beagles can get the job done without scaring people.

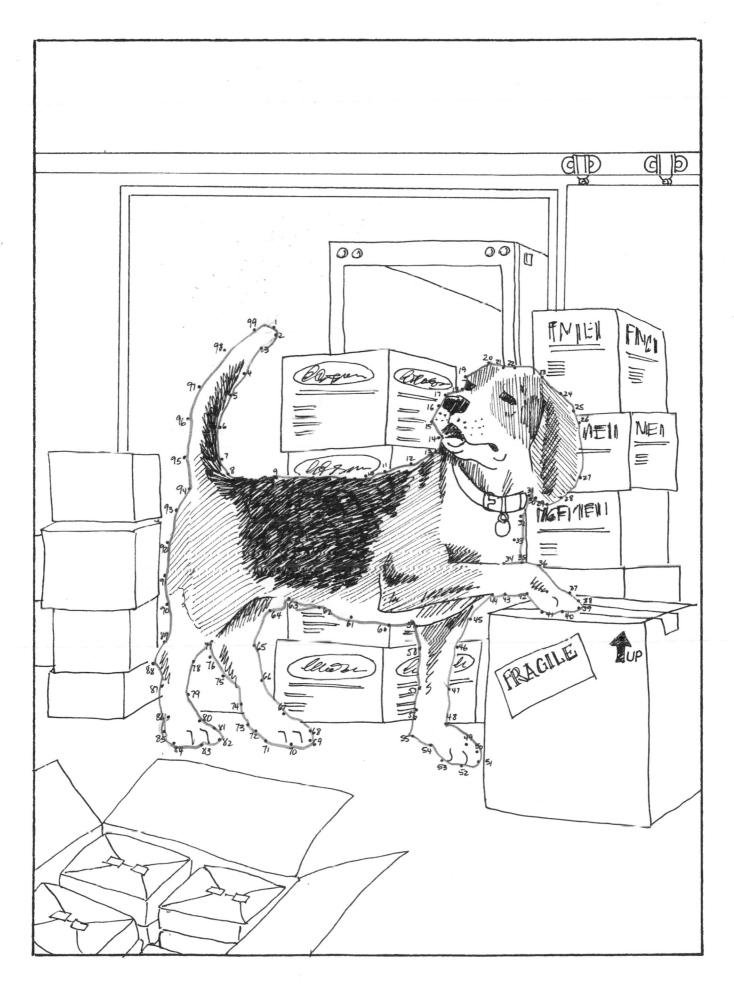

BEDLINGTON TERRIER

ORIGIN: Great Britain, around 1825

SIZE: 15–17 inches (38–43cm) tall; weighing 17–23 pounds (8–10kg)

APPEARANCE: Thick, wooly coats that tend to curl, especially on face and head; rounded head with top knot; arched back

These wire-coated terriers were crosses of Whippets and Dandie Dinmont Terriers, often called "Gypsy Dogs" because they traveled with Gypsy caravans. Gypsies found that Bedlingtons, which look uncannily like innocent lambs, made ideal poaching assistants. The breed traces back to the small town of Bedlington in the English Midland.

The Bedlington was developed as a sort of "all-purpose" dog that could catch an otter in the water, run down a rabbit in the field, or hold its own in a dogfight. Although only a medium-sized dog at most, Bedlingtons are willing to tackle prey like badgers and foxes that outmatch them in size and weight.

DID YOU KNOW? The old phrase "a wolf in sheep's clothing" originated as a reference to the Bedlington.

BLOODHOUND

ORIGIN:	Belgium, around AD 800
SIZE:	23–27 inches (58–69cm) tall; weighing 80–110 pounds (36–50kg), occasionally as much as 130 pounds (59kg) or more
APPEARANCE:	Double-chin-like dewlap under jaw; wrinkled forehead that gives a perpetually mournful expression

Supposedly, a monk named Hubert (later Saint Hubert) brought a hound of this type back to Belgium from the Middle East after the Crusades. Bloodhounds are still sometimes called Saint Hubert Hounds. They were never called Bloodhounds because they were fierce or bloodthirsty, although Hollywood movies have given them that reputation. They were, rather, "dogs of the blood" or dogs owned by people of noble blood.

Bloodhounds have a keen sense of smell; they can follow a trail more than two weeks old, scenting the ground, not the air, and have been known to relentlessly pursue a scent for over 100 miles (161km). Friendly and responsive, these dogs are also determined and persistent.

DID YOU KNOW? Bloodhounds are the only breed of dog whose testimony (evidence they discover by following a scent) is legally admissible in every U.S. court of law.

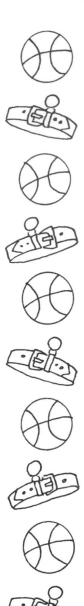

BORDER COLLIE

ORIGIN:	Great Britain, 1700s
SIZE:	18–21 inches (46–54cm) tall; weighing 30–45 pounds (14–20kg)
APPEARANCE:	Dense, shiny coats, commonly black and white; semi-erect ears flopping over at tips

These hardworking dogs will herd anything from people to pigs. Because they were largely used and developed in the border areas of Scotland, England, and Wales, these highly intelligent little dynamos were called Border Collies.

Border Collies usually herd sheep, but the U.S. Fish & Wildlife Service has used them in recent years to save an endangered species of bird known as the Aleutian goose. In one instance, biologists spent three frustrating weeks rounding up a mere 120 birds. Then Lass and Cap, two Border Collies, were brought in, and rounded up 145 geese in just four days. Thanks to Lass and Cap, Aleutian geese now inhabit most of their former habitat.

DID YOU KNOW? A Border Collie named Jet works at the Southwest Florida International Airport, clearing the tarmac of cranes, egrets, herons, and grackles, saving the U.S. civil aviation industry an estimated $300 million in damages.

BOXER

ORIGIN: Germany, 1800s

SIZE: 21–25 inches (54–64cm) tall; weighing 60–70 pounds (27–32kg)

APPEARANCE: Squarish snouts; drop ears

Mastiff-type dogs, but leaner and more agile, Boxers are playful and affectionate dogs. Their drop ears are often cropped so they look pricked, but this practice is gradually falling out of favor. Although this breed was developed as a fighting dog, it is gentle enough that it is used as a Seeing Eye dog.

Boxers were meant to be a refined version of the old "bullen beisser" (bull-baiter), streamlined in body and sweetened in temperament. They may look ready for a fight, but they usually prefer a kiss.

DID YOU KNOW? A boxer named Mathias was awarded the Iron Cross for heroism during World War II. A German war dog, Mathias is credited with rescuing 17 wounded German soldiers by delivering their call for reinforcements. He later succumbed to his injuries.

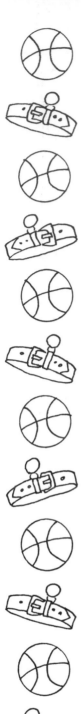
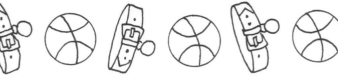

CAIRN TERRIER

ORIGIN:	Scotland, 1500s
SIZE:	10–12 inches (25–30cm) tall; weighing 13–16 pounds (6–7kg)
APPEARANCE:	Small pricked ears; long tail held high; shaggy, dense, double-layered, water-resistant coat; small, dark hazel eyes with bushy eyebrows

Developed to seek out vermin that invaded the small mounds of rocks (called "cairns") used to mark property boundaries and graves, Cairn Terriers are excellent swimmers and compulsive diggers. Very bold for its size, the Cairn Terrier was used to hunt not only rats and mice, but also foxes, badgers, and other animals larger than the dog itself. Often described as "cheeky," the Cairn's expression is sometimes called "foxlike."

DID YOU KNOW? Scots placed such a high value on these affectionate little dogs that when James VI sent six Cairnlike terriers to the king of France as a gift in 1600, he divided the group in two and sent them on different ships, to ensure that some would survive the voyage.

CANAAN DOG

ORIGIN: Middle East, as far back as 2200 BC

SIZE: 19–24 inches (48–61cm); weighing 35–55
                    pounds (16–25kg)

APPEARANCE: Short coat; pricked ears; bushy tail that
                    curves over the back

This Spitz-type dog dates back to the beginnings of Judaism, Islam, and Christianity. Its ancestors were feral (or pariah) dogs. They were domesticated primarily to protect the flocks of goats and camels belonging to Bedouin tribes from attack by desert jackals.

These intelligent and resourceful desert dwellers are alert, easy to train, devoted to their owners, and wary of strangers. Sturdy, long-lived dogs, Canaans often continue to work into their teens. They have hard pads on their feet to help them walk on hot sand. They have also adapted to desert life in other ways: Canaans can survive on less water than other breeds and can cool themselves down more quickly than most other dogs.

DID YOU KNOW? The national dog of Israel, Canaans work as guide dogs for the blind, police dogs, and search-and-rescue dogs. They are particularly sought after to guard communal Israeli settlements called *kibbutzim*.

CAVALIER KING CHARLES SPANIEL

ORIGIN: Japan, about 2,000 years ago, and 1920s United States

SIZE: 12–13 inches (30–33cm) tall; weighing 18–25 pounds (4–8kg)

APPEARANCE: Long ears; large, expressive eyes; shaggy coat; long, feathered tail

The King Charles Spaniel traces its ancestry back 2,000 years to Japan. Its popularity soared when it became the favorite pet of British king Charles II (1630–1685), who was often accused of ignoring affairs of state to play with his dogs. As time went on, the original, long-snouted dog was crossbred with smaller oriental dogs to get a smaller and ever smaller canine.

In the 1920's, an American dog fancier offered a rich reward to anyone who could breed a good example of the type of dog seen in the royal portraits of the Renaissance. The word *cavalier* was added to distinguish this "new old" dog from the smaller, flat-faced dog it had become.

A particularly friendly and obedient dog, the Cavalier is social and seeks affection from everyone it meets.

DID YOU KNOW? King Charles II made a royal decree that all spaniels of this variety could go anywhere they pleased, including shops, churches, and even into sessions of Parliament, where his dogs had their own chairs in the House of Lords.

CHOW CHOW

ORIGIN: Asia, millions of years ago.

SIZE: 18–22 inches (46–56cm) tall, weighing 45–70 pounds (22–32kg).

APPEARANCE: Noted for magnificent mane of fur around its head

Chows trace their lineage back to an early wild dog called *Canis palustris*, dating back millions of years. These unusual dogs were once used in northern Asia as multipurpose dogs: guarding herds, hunting game, and working as watchdogs. They were also harnessed as sled dogs. Their coats were shaved to make fur garments for human beings, and the dog, as a puppy, was considered deliciously edible (with a taste like lamb), and able to confer strength and courage on any who ate its flesh.

British sailors called them "chow," an old slang word referring to extra stuff packed into the hold of a ship for the journey back to England.

Although Chows are considered aloof with strangers, they are fiercely loyal to their owners and are very alert, independent, and courageous. Fearsome fighters, they're unlikely to do battles unless it's forced on them.

DID YOU KNOW? The Chow has a blue-black tongue. It is the only dog besides the Shar-Pei to have a tongue of that color.

DALMATIAN

ORIGIN: Probably Croatia, 1400s

SIZE: 22–24 inches (56–61cm) tall; weighing 30–55 pounds (14–25kg)

APPEARANCE: Sleek white coat with well-defined black spots.

Named for Dalmatia (what is now Croatia), these dogs may have been brought from India by Gypsies, but Dalmatians are generally considered to have come from the former Yugoslavia in the 1400s. Dalmatians are a cross between pointers and hounds, although they have never been used for hunting or scent work.

This breed has always been good around horses, having a calming effect on them, unlike other breeds that make their hoofed friends nervous. In the 1800s, "Dals" were frequently seen trotting beside and under aristocratic horse-drawn hansom cabs. Dalmatians were especially valuable for their work in clearing the way for onrushing horse-drawn fire engines in the 19th and early 20th centuries, and many firehouses today still use these alert and lively dog as mascots. Boisterous and energetic, Dalmatians have incredible endurance and can travel at a moderate pace almost indefinitely.

DID YOU KNOW? All Dalmatian puppies are pure white at birth. Spots begin to fill in after about three weeks.

DINGO

ORIGIN: Australia, 1450 BC

SIZE: 21 inches (53cm) tall; weighing
                     22–44 pounds(10–20kg)

APPEARANCE: Short hair, pricked ears, long tail; most
                     are yellow-ginger or tawny brown, with
                     white-tipped tails

The Dingo was a domesticated pet and helpmate to the Aboriginal inhabitants of Australia. In the wide-open spaces of the Outback, with no real predators as competition, the dog spread out and became feral to the point that it is now considered a wild dog, although still a breed. In fact, it is considered the oldest pure breed of dog in the world. Its teeth are more wolflike than doglike, and it howls, but barks very little. It became a sensation when first exhibited at the London Zoo in 1828 as "the Australian Dog."

Today, Dingoes are often trained as hunting dogs. Unlike most wolves and dogs, they are solitary animals and do not usually hunt in packs.

DID YOU KNOW? The world's longest fence is the Dingo Barrier Fence, which stretches almost 5,000 miles (8,000km) across Australia. Its purpose is to protect sheep from the Dingoes that roam the Outback.

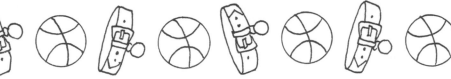

DOBERMAN PINSCHER

ORIGIN:	Germany, 1890
SIZE:	25–27 inches (64–69cm) tall; weighing 66–88 pounds (30–40kg)
APPEARANCE:	Usually black and tan; sleek coated; drop ears that are sometimes cropped; long tails that are usually docked

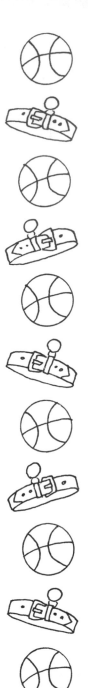

This dog was "invented" by a tax collector named Louis Dobermann, who lived in Germany in 1890. Herr Dobermann also happened to run the local pound, so he had access to a wide variety of dogs. He created his own personal guardian, mixing in German Shepherd for hardiness and intelligence; German Pinscher for quick, terrierlike reflexes; Weimar Pointer for a fine nose; Rottweiler for strength; Greyhound for speed; and Manchester Terrier for sleekness. The result was a bold and fearless dog that quickly gained a reputation for aggressiveness.

Dobermans have strong guarding instincts, but they can make reliable family pets if properly trained from puppyhood. They also have a reputation for tasting everything they run across, and—ironically for such a carnivorous-looking dog—are fond of many vegetables.

DID YOU KNOW? Although the bulldog is the mascot of the U.S. Marine Corps, the Doberman is the official "Marine War Dog."

GERMAN SHEPHERD

ORIGIN:	Germany, seventh century
SIZE:	23–25 inches (58–64cm) tall; weighing 75–95 pounds (34–43kg)
APPEARANCE:	Usually a black-and-tan shaggy coat; pricked ears; long tail

Developed in Germany in the seventh century for sheepherding, German Shepherds are considered to be direct descendants of the Bronze Age wolf. Among the world's most popular dogs, they're both versatile and intelligent. Enthusiastic workers, shepherds have long been used as war dogs, police dogs, Seeing Eye dogs, and for search-and-rescue work. "Buddy," the very first Seeing Eye dog in the United States, began guiding his blind master in the 1920s.

DID YOU KNOW? Rin Tin Tin, aka Rinty, was a real German Shepherd born in a trench in France during World War I. Rinty became a messenger dog and was even wounded in battle. After the war, he came home a hero and went Hollywood, making 22 black-and-white films.

GOLDEN RETRIEVER

ORIGIN:	Great Britain, 1800s
SIZE:	21–24 inches (53–61cm) tall; weighing 55–75 pounds (25–34kg)
APPEARANCE:	Medium-thick, water-repellant coat in shades of pale yellow to gold

Although some people believe these shiny beauties are descended from Russian circus dogs, it's more likely the Golden is a cross between the Flat-Coated Retriever, Labrador Retriever, and Irish Setter, bred to emphasize the gene that produces a light yellow or golden color.

In 19th-century England, Golden Retrievers were used as hunting companions to retrieve game birds. They were created as gundogs (dogs that are not scared by the sound of gunfire), versatile enough to be speedy on both land and in the water. They are gentle dogs with a tender, intelligent facial expression that sets them apart from many breeds.

DID YOU KNOW? A Golden Retriever named Shanda was elected mayor of Guthrie, Colorado, in the early 1990s. The tiny town couldn't get state funding for a stoplight at its main intersection. After Shanda was elected, the town got so much national publicity, it got its stoplight and many other municipal improvements.

41

GREYHOUND

ORIGIN: Egypt, 5000 BC

SIZE: 27–30 inches (69–76cm) tall; weighing 60–70 pounds (27–32kg)

APPEARANCE: Sleek and streamlined; sharp muzzle; broad chest with increased lung capacity for running

This coursing dog is one of history's oldest breeds, dating back to Ancient Egypt. Images of greyhounds (as well as greyhound mummies) have been found in Egyptian tombs and pyramids. The dogs were first brought to Europe by Phoenician traders, and immediately became a favorite of European nobility.

Gentle by nature, racing greyhounds wear muzzles only because the excitement of the race can make them nervous and nippy. These are friendly, lively dogs that make great pets, even if you walk and never run them. Greyhounds are sight hounds, following their prey by sight rather than smell.

You will never find a gray greyhound. The name is derived from the Old English word *grach*, which means "dog."

DID YOU KNOW? Greyhounds have been clocked over short distances at 43.5 miles (70km) per hour, and can outrun deer, foxes, and rabbits.

IRISH WOLFHOUND

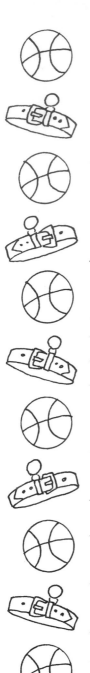

ORIGIN: Ireland, around 100 BC

SIZE: 28–33 inches (71–84cm) tall; weighing 99–120 pounds (45–54kg)

APPEARANCE: Tall with a rough, shaggy coat

Few dogs, alone, are any match for a wolf. Irish Wolfhounds are among the very few canines that have a chance of winning if fighting head-to-head with a wolf. Considered the world's biggest dog in terms of height, these canine giants were once used to hunt wolves in Ireland. They were considered royal dogs of ancient lineage, but almost became extinct in the 1800s when all the wolves in Ireland had been killed and there were none left for the dog to hunt.

A popular folktale tells of the faithful Irish Wolfhound Gelert, companion to the Prince of Wales in the early 1200s. When Prince Llewellyn went hunting one day, he left Gelert guarding his baby. He returned to find the dog, stained with blood, standing by the cradle. In a rage, Llewellyn killed Gelert with his sword. Only then did he discover the dead body of a wolf on the other side of the cradle, next to the prince's unharmed child.

DID YOU KNOW? Nicknamed "the Gentle Giant," the Irish Wolfhound is the official national dog of Ireland.

JACK RUSSELL TERRIER

ORIGIN: England, 1800s

SIZE: 14 inches (36cm) tall; weighing 16–18 pounds (7–9kg)

APPEARANCE: Can be smooth or rough coated, but coats are always double-layered and waterproof.

The Reverend Jack Russell, nicknamed "the Hunting Parson" in his parish in Devon, England, wanted a hunting dog that could keep up with the horses, instead of being slung over the saddle while the fox chase was on (as most terriers were). So, he crossed small working terriers with longer-legged dogs to get a long-legged terrier fast enough to run with the hunting hounds. Jack Russells proved to be quick, both physically and mentally. About the size of a fox, they won't hesitate to go down a hole after anything they're chasing.

DID YOU KNOW? Jack Russell Terriers are not officially recognized by either the British or American Kennel Club—because their owners don't want them to be. Jack Russell fanciers say setting standards would prissy up and ruin this independent, personable dog.

LUNDEHUND

ORIGIN:	Norway, 1500s
SIZE:	12–15 inches (30–38cm) tall; weighing 13–14 pounds (6–6.5kg)
APPEARANCE:	Short, rough coat; six toes

Developed as a puffin-hunting dog, this unusual dog has six toes, instead of the usual four, to aid it in scaling the cliffs where puffins nest. The Lundehund is such an agile dog, it can bend its head horizontally backwards almost far enough to touch its back (but don't try this at home!). It is the only dog that can close its ears to keep water out.

DID YOU KNOW? At one point, as puffins grew scarce and became less of a food source for Nordic farmers, there were only 50 Lundehunds left. A breed rescue push was launched to save this distinctive Scandinavian pooch.

MUTT
(MONGREL, MIXED BREED, AND "HEINZ 57")

ORIGIN: Mutts are puppies that come from the mating of two different breeds, a breed and a mutt, or two mutts

SIZE AND APPEARANCE: Mutts come in all shapes and sizes

Some dog lovers look with scorn on highly specialized, pedigreed dogs, calling them artificial and pointing out that some recognized breeds have special medical problems because they've been taken to the extreme (face too flat, legs too short, and so on) People who prefer mutts believe their dogs will have the benefit of the attributes of all the breeds in their ancestry.

It's hard to determine the size and shape of most mutts until they are full grown. In general, puppies with big feet will grow into big dogs, and pups with heavy fur on their bellies will have thick, shaggy coats. The exceptionally intelligent Poodle is, by far, the most popular dog to cross. Odd mixes include the the Doxie-Poo (Dachshund and Miniature Poodle), the Rott-a-Dor (Rottweiler and Labrador), and the Bullpug (Bulldog and Pug).

DID YOU KNOW? A Schnauzer–Siberian Husky mix named Ginny was chosen "Cat of the Year" in 1998 by the Westchester Feline Club in New York for rescuing and protecting stray cats.

NEWFOUNDLAND

ORIGIN: Newfoundland, Canada, 1700s

SIZE: 26–28 inches (66–71cm) tall; weighing
                110–150 pounds (50–68kg)

APPEARANCE: Thick, insulating undercoat, oily, highly
                water-resistant outer coat

First bred to help fishermen haul in their nets, Newfoundlands are excellent swimmers. They are also very responsive and gentle dogs, eager to help humans, even at the risk of their own lives.

On December 10, 1919, the steamship *Ethie* left Port Saunders in Newfoundland, Canada, headed for Saint John's Harbor with 92 passengers and crew on board. Caught in a sudden winter gale, the ship was pitched onto the jagged rock. No lifeboat could get through the huge breakers to bring a lifeline to the sinking ship. It was a Newfoundland that finally swam through the storm, carrying a cable, which was hooked to a boatswain's chair, so people could be levered by pulley to shore. Thanks to that courageous Newfoundland (which also survived), not a single life was lost.

DID YOU KNOW? A Newfoundland named Seaman was employed by the Lewis & Clark Corps of Discovery in the early 19th century.

PEKINGESE

ORIGIN: China, several thousand years ago

SIZE: 6–9 inches (15–23cm) tall, weighing 7–12 pounds (3–5kg)

APPEARANCE: Wide-set dropped ears; long, silky coat; flat face

In Ancient China, Pekingese were exclusively the dogs of emperors. These tiny "lion dogs" first came west in 1860 when British troops looted and burned the emperor's summer palace at Peking (now called Beijing). Five of the dogs were found still alive in the women's apartment wing of the palace and were taken back to England. One, nicknamed Looty, was presented to Queen Victoria.

The Pekingese has been bred in the image of the Buddhist symbol of the lion, ears that give the impression of a mane. Independent and lively, the Peke, despite its small size, makes a good watchdog. But this is very much a lap dog, affectionate and loyal.

DID YOU KNOW? A Pekingese named Sun Yat Sen, owned by American publisher Henry Sleeper Harper, was among the 3 dogs (out of the 10 or so dogs known to have sailed) on the Titanic to survive the sinking. He escaped in the lap of his owner in Lifeboat Number Three.

PERUVIAN INCA ORCHID

ORIGIN: Peru, 1200s

SIZE: 15–20 inches (38–50cm) tall; weighing
                   20–38 pounds (9–17kg)

APPEARANCE: Nearly hairless; deerlike in structure
                   and movement; light boned, lithe, and
                   swift; pricked ears

The Orchid was developed mainly for use as a bed warmer. The name of this dog comes from the Inca tradition of keeping the animals inside all day, in rooms decorated with orchids. The Orchid spends most of its time outside at night, so it is also called the Moonflower Dog or *Perro Flora*.

Orchids are hairless, except for a shock of hair on the top of the head that looks a little like a hairpiece. With their mottled skin on a pink or white background, these dogs need constant oiling so their skin won't dry out. They also need to be kept out of the sun to avoid sunburn. Orchid dogs are missing their premolars, which often causes their tongues to hang out the sides of their mouths.

DID YOU KNOW? In the language of the Peruvian Oeuchua tribe, this dog is called *Caa-allepo*, which translates to "dog without clothes."

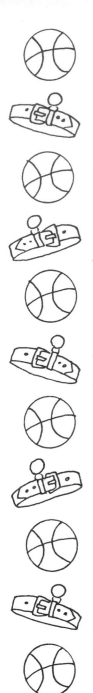
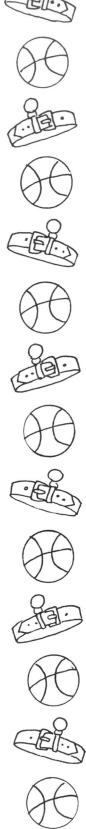

PIT BULL

ORIGIN:	Great Britain, 1500s
SIZE:	18–22 inches (46–56cm) tall; weighing 50–80 pounds (23–36kg)
APPEARANCE:	Usually white, often with a black patch of fur around one eye; compact and muscular, with particularly strong jaws

The Staffordshire Bull Terrier of England was bred from bulldogs, terriers, and the Roman Molossus warrior dog, which went into battle dressed in spiked armor and carrying spears on its back. In the 16th through 19th centuries, these dogs were used in bear-and bull-baiting contests, sporting events where spectators would watch the animals fight, often to the death, and bet on the outcome.

The most feared and legislated-against dog in the world today (in some states it is not legal to own a Pit Bull), these dogs are not "born bad." Pit Bulls raised properly with love and affection are trustworthy, intelligent, and particularly loyal pets.

DID YOU KNOW? The Pit Bull was the breed that symbolized U.S. patriotism in posters and ads during World War I.

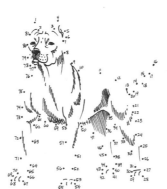

POODLE

ORIGIN:	Germany, 1400s
SIZE:	Standard Poodle, 15–19 inches (38–48cm) tall, weighing 45–70 pounds (20–32kg); Miniature, 11 inches (28cm) tall, 26–30 pounds (12–14kg); Toy, 9 inches (23cm), 15 pounds (7kg)
APPEARANCE:	Dense, woolly hair solid in color (black, white, reddish-brown or gray); wide, drooped ears and docked tail

Poodles were bred for retrieving game from rivers and marshland. Their distinctive haircuts began as a way to provide warmth around the dog's ankle joints; the front mane was for buoyancy, almost like a life preserver. Although the Poodle's distinctive cut may have begun for practical purposes, French queen Marie Antoinette is usually credited for the famous "lion clip" of today's show dogs. She wanted her poodles to match the livery of her servants, who wore puffy shirts and frilly cuffs. Poodle fur is sometimes dyed pink, blue, or other colors, and festooned with pom-poms and ribbons.

DID YOU KNOW? Prince Rupert of the Rhine had his Poodle, Boy, sit in on royal council meetings, and often turned to the dog for advice. Boy was killed in 1644 as he fought alongside his master in the English Civil War.

PORTUGUESE WATER DOG

ORIGIN: Algarve, Portugal, 1500s

SIZE: 16–22 inches (41–56cm); weighing 35–55 pounds (16–25kg)

APPEARANCE: Long, wavy coat; tail curls loosely over back, with thick plume at tip

Developed by fishermen on Portugal's southern coast, these obedient, friendly dogs had many uses before the development of modern technology. Keen eyesight let them spot shoals of fish before anyone else on the boat; they retrieved any equipment that fell overboard, diving deeply when necessary, and carried messages between fishing boats.

Also known as the *Cao de Aqua*, the breed came close to dying out in the 1960s, when only 50 remained. Radar and other 20th-century fishing techniques rendered this specialized dog obsolete. However, the movement to save the breed was successful, and today it is a popular companion dog in Europe and the United States.

DID YOU KNOW? "Porties" have webbed toes. Wonderful swimmers, they can actually "herd" fish into a net, as well as carry a fish so gently that the dog's teeth never even break the fish's skin.

SAINT BERNARD

ORIGIN: Switzerland, 900s

SIZE: 24–28 inches (61–71cm) tall; weighing
                     110–200 pounds (50–91kg)

APPEARANCE: Thick fur, broad square head, drop ears,
                     long tail, very pronounced jowls; most
                     often white-and-tan fur

This thick-furred teddy bear of a dog is descended from the giant (and now extinct) Roman Molossus dogs, used to guard mountain passes into Italy. Bernard of Methon (later known as Saint Bernard) established a hospice in one such pass in the 10th century to aid people making holy pilgrimages to Rome. He trained the Molossus descendants to find and rescue travelers lost in avalanches and blizzards. By the mid-18th century, the monks at the abbey of Saint Bernard had crossed the original Molossus-type dog with Great Danes, for height, and Bloodhounds, for scenting ability. In the 19th century, Newfoundland genes went into the mix to provide a thicker, insulating coat. Experts have estimated that Saint Bernard–type dogs have saved at least 2,000 lives since they began their work as Good Samaritans.

DID YOU KNOW? The biggest Saint Bernard on record weighed in at 295 pounds.

RESCUE

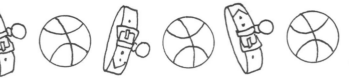

SHAR-PEI

ORIGIN:	China, about 2,000 years ago
SIZE:	18–20 inches (46–51cm) tall; weighing 35–45 pounds (16–20kg)
APPEARANCE:	Loose, wrinkled skin; bristly coat; tiny, dropped ears; broad snout

Created from a mix of Chows and Han dynasty (206 BC–AD 220) dogs, these unusual canines were bred to guard noblemen and to fight in sporting events. Their loose skin made it hard for an opponent to get a firm grip; in fact, the skin on a young Shar-Pei is so loose that it is able to turn on its opponent and bite, even when its rival has the Shar-Pei's own flesh firmly grasped in its teeth. Some Shar-Peis can literally turn around backward in their own skins.

Adult Shar-Peis usually grow into their coats, with wrinkles confined to the face and shoulders. Prone to skin and eye diseases, these loyal but aloof dogs have blue-black tongues, like Chows, and also share the Chow's independent spirit.

DID YOU KNOW? In the second half of the 20th century, Chinese Communist leaders opposed the existence of domestic dogs, calling them an emblem of Western triviality and decadence. The Shar-Pei was almost wiped out. Since then, the breed has made a comeback.

SHIBA INU

ORIGIN: Japan, 500 BC

SIZE: 14–16 inches (36–41cm) tall; weighing 20–30 pounds (9–14kg)

APPEARANCE: Pricked ears; tightly curled tail; sturdy; thick coated

These small, terrierlike dogs were developed in Japan centuries ago to hunt small game. *Shiba Inu* translates from Japanese into "small dog." They seem to have an almost eager expression, always ready for action. Although the Shiba Inu rarely barks, it sometimes makes a sort of strange shrieking call—neither a howl nor a yodel.

Without question this is the most popular of Japan's native dog breeds. Independent and industrious, the Shiba is used little for hunting these days, but mainly as a companion or guard dog. The Shiba came so close to extinction in the 1920s, following World War I, that Japan has now declared the breed a natural monument.

DID YOU KNOW? Because little of Japan's rental housing allows dogs, dog-loving Japanese citizens have established dog rental parks, where the Shiba Inu is the most frequently rented breed. Young white-collar professionals often use a dog walk as an icebreaker on a first date.

SIBERIAN HUSKY

ORIGIN: Siberia, 1800s

SIZE: 20–24 inches (51–61cm) tall; weighing 35–60 pounds (16–27kg)

APPEARANCE: Dense woolly undercoat protected by tough outer guard hairs; pricked ears; long bushy tail; eyes often blue

Developed in the 1800s by the Chukchi tribe along the Kolyma River region of Siberia, the first Huskies were imported to Alaska in 1909. These legendary sled dogs of the tundra are tireless workers and the most dependable form of transportation in the Arctic and Antarctic regions. They don't bark much, but are prone to communal howling.

The most famous of all Huskies is Balto, the lead dog in the lifesaving marathon run in 1925 to deliver diphtheria serum from Anchorage to Nome, Alaska—a distance of 671 miles (1,080 km). Balto led his team through blizzards in temperatures as low as 57°F (49°C) below freezing. A famous sled dog race called the Iditarod has been run annually since the early 1970s, honoring—and doubling—Balto's run.

DID YOU KNOW? In 1911, Roald Amundsen became the first man to reach the South Pole, thanks mainly to the aid of his 52 Siberian Huskies.

SPITZ

ORIGIN:	Fossils date back 5,000 years
SIZE:	14–19 inches (36–48cm) tall; weighing 18–35 pounds (8–16kg); also comes in miniature and toy sizes
APPEARANCE:	Long, snow white fur; "smiling" facial expression

The Spitz is one of the most basic breed "styles" of dog. Both tiny Pomeranians and large Chow Chows are considered "Spitz-type" dogs. The first Spitz was a Nordic herding dog, used to herd reindeer and sometimes to pull sleds. The breed came to Germany by way of the Vikings, who were looting and plundering Europe in the 1200s. The American Spitz is descended from German Spitz dogs and is sometimes called "the American Eskimo" because of its white fur.

Hardy and long lived, the Spitz is a natural watchdog, tending to bark if there is something wrong or unusual. The harsh-textured coat is "self-cleaning," which means it easily shakes off dirt or mud when dry. A dense wool undercoat keeps the dog from getting cold in northern weather, and you are more likely to find this canine curled up outside in a snowbank than in a doghouse. Often used in dog circus acts, the Spitz also makes a fine family companion and watchdog.

DID YOU KNOW? A Spitz named Nori foiled a kidnapping in 1992 by biting the abductor firmly in the seat of his pants.

XOLOITZCUINTLI
(XOLO; PRONOUNCED SHOLO-ITS-QUINTLI)

ORIGIN: Ancient Mexico

SIZE: 23–25 inches (58–64cm) tall; weighing 40–60 pounds (18–27kg)

APPEARANCE: Dark, wrinkled skin; usually has sparse tufts of hair on the top of its head and the lower part of its tail

Xolotl was the Aztec god of twins and ball games, and he had a companion dog named Xolo. In the Nahuatl tribe's language, *Xolo* means "bald dog." An indigenous Mexican mutation of a wild dog, the Xolo dates back to the beginnings of the ancient Aztec civilization.

The naked skin of the Xolo is warm to the touch, and the dog was used as a healer, pressing its warmth to painful parts of a human body. Aztec medicine men believed the dog "drew out the pain," and could cure headaches, asthma, rheumatism, aching muscles, insomnia, and malaria. Of course, it couldn't really cure any diseases, but it did make a great hot-water bottle on a cold night, and was also an alert and protective watchdog. Calm, dignified, and obedient, Xolos are wary of strangers.

DID YOU KNOW? The same gene that causes the Xolo to be hairless affects its dentition, so Xolos have fewer teeth than most dogs.

YORKSHIRE TERRIER

ORIGIN: Great Britain, Middle Ages

SIZE: 9–10 inches (23–25cm) tall; weighing 6–8 pounds (3–4kg)

APPEARANCE: Large pricked ears; silky, steel-blue, tan-marked coat that sometimes reaches the ground

In the Middle Ages, the king of England decreed that a peasant could not own a dog over a certain (rather small) size. The peasants therefore began breeding small, but still fierce and feisty dogs. This was the start of all terriers or "earth" dogs, which fearlessly tackle not only rabbits and grouse, but also foxes and badgers and other large animals. One such terrier developed into the Yorkshire Terrier or "Yorkie." In the 1800s, selective breeding shrank the already small dog to an easy-to-carry arm ornament for the gentry.

Grooming for a show dog's long coat includes setting or wrapping it in rollers. A Yorkie often needs its silky fur tied back in a topknot, so its dainty face can be seen.

DID YOU KNOW? In 19th-century England, "ratting" competitions were all the craze. Small dogs were placed in a ring to kill as many rats as possible in a set time period. Little Yorkies often won large purses at these matches.

INDEX